Help a Friend

DISABILITY

QUICK REFERENCE GUIDE

ENCOURAGEMENT FROM GOD'S WORD

WHAT TO SAY AND DO

HOW TO HELP

COMPANION TO THE *BEYOND SUFFERING BIBLE*

Help a Friend

DISABILITY

A DISABILITY is a physical or mental impairment that substantially limits one or more of a person's major life activities.[1] It can be present at birth or come about in a moment of crisis, such as an accident or injury, or it can emerge over time, such as a visual impairment or multiple sclerosis. It may be short-term or long-term, and it may include physical or intellectual impairments (or both).

While each individual with disabilities faces unique challenges, they all have one thing in common: they are *people first*. They experience the same joy, fear, sadness, and love as everyone else. They want to be valued members of the community and to participate in life to the best of their abilities. And they all have a great deal to teach about the important things in life.

[1] Americans with Disabilities Act of 1990, Title 42, Chapter 126, Section 12102, Definitions.

Disability Facts

- **82+ MILLION AMERICANS** have a disability or chronic illness.
- **1 IN 5 PEOPLE** in the U.S. lives with some type of disability.
- **10 MILLION PEOPLE** a year experience a serious mental illness.
- **ROUGHLY 65 MILLION AMERICANS** provide care for someone with a disability or chronic illness.
- **4.5 MILLION VETERANS** received disability benefits in 2015.
- **THE 2010 U.S. CENSUS** reported that 5.2 million children under age 15 had a disability, with about half of those classified as severe disabilities.

Going Deeper

- **BEYOND SUFFERING: A CHRISTIAN VIEW ON DISABILITY MINISTRY** is a groundbreaking course from the Christian Institute on Disability that is transforming how Christians view God's plan for disability and suffering. Available as a certificate program or for college credit! www.joniandfriends.org/BYS/

The *Beyond Suffering Bible* is the first topical Bible written for those who suffer and the people who love them. Joni Eareckson Tada and the experts at Joni and Friends' Christian Institute on Disability provide uplifting insights that move us beyond the "why" of suffering. This Bible helps readers take hold of the eternal value God is building into our lives, especially as we find ourselves in the valleys of life. For more information visit beyondsufferingbible.com.

HARDCOVER 978-1-4143-9202-8
SOFTCOVER 978-1-4143-9558-6
BROWN/TAN DELUXE LEATHERLIKE 978-1-4143-9559-3
BROWN/TAN DELUXE LEATHERLIKE (indexed) 978-1-4143-9560-9
TEAL/BROWN/ROSE GOLD LEATHERLIKE 978-1-4143-9561-6
TEAL/BROWN/ROSE GOLD LEATHERLIKE (indexed) 978-1-4143-9562-3

- **JONI AND FRIENDS INTERNATIONAL DISABILITY CENTER** is dedicated to extending the love and message of Jesus Christ to people who are affected by disability around the world. www.joniandfriends.org
- **YOUNG LIFE CAPERNAUM** offers creative Christian programs for students and young adults with disabilities. www.younglife.org/ForEveryKid/Capernaum
- **DISABILITY.GOV** provides quick and easy access to comprehensive information about disability programs, services, laws, and benefits. www.disability.gov
- **NATIONAL ORGANIZATION ON DISABILITY** (NOD) is a private, non-profit organization that promotes the full participation and contributions of America's 56 million people with disabilities in all aspects of life. NOD focuses on increasing employment opportunities for the 80 percent of working-age Americans with disabilities who are not employed. www.nod.org
- **THE NATIONAL COUNCIL ON INDEPENDENT LIVING** advances independent living and the rights of people with disabilities. NCIL envisions a world in which people with disabilities are valued equally and participate fully. www.ncil.org

Friendship Looks Beyond Disability

IN ADDITION to whatever loss might be occasioned by the disability itself, people with disabilities often experience an even greater sense of loss as a result of the attitudes and discrimination they encounter in society. Friends become especially important when society marginalizes a person who cannot function in the usual, expected ways. You have the opportunity to be the "hands and feet" of Jesus simply by being a true friend.

A true friend looks beyond a person's disability and recognizes the God-given gifts of another. The deepest friendships are forged in the fire of adversity. They are mutually beneficial, affirming, and dependable. When darkness threatens to overtake us, a friend holds the light at the end of the tunnel that beckons us forward.

"But What Do I Say?"

- **A NEW DISABILITY** or a new level of impairment will require time for adjustment. Show patience and support without implying timelines or an attitude that your friend "should be getting it together" by now.
- **RESPECT** personal boundaries and inquire about your friend's desired level of help and assistance rather than acting on assumptions.
- **DON'T TALK** to someone with a physical disability as if they are also intellectually impaired. Just because your friend's body has been impacted by a disability doesn't mean she is any less capable of comprehension. Talk to your friend as you would anyone else.
- **HAVE A** sense of humor and don't be surprised when your friend with a disability does too! We all need to be able to laugh at ourselves, so reflect an appropriate light-hearted attitude, especially when it comes to social skills.
- **FRIENDSHIP** is reciprocal. Be honest about your own struggles and joys of life, letting your friend have a better understanding of who you are and an opportunity to minister to you when necessary.
- **SPEAK DIRECTLY** to your friend! Look him in the eye and talk to him, rather than to a family member or caregiver who may be present.

Books and Online Resources

- ***EXPRESSING FAITH IN JESUS: CHURCH MEMBERSHIP FOR PEOPLE WITH INTELLECTUAL DISABILITIES,* BY RONALD C. VREDEVELD** (Grand Rapids, MI: Faith Alive Christian Resources, 2005). Available at www.faithaliveresources.org.
- ***INCLUDING PEOPLE WITH DISABILITIES IN FAITH COMMUNITIES,* BY ERIK W. CARTER** (Baltimore, MD: Brookes Publishing, 2007). This book addresses how congregations, families, and service providers can work together to support the full participation of individuals with disabilities in the faith community. www.joniandfriends.org/store/
- ***LIFE IN THE BALANCE: BIBLICAL ANSWERS FOR THE ISSUES OF OUR DAY,* BY JONI EARECKSON TADA AND FRIENDS** (Grand Rapids, MI: Regal, 2010). This study, for use by individuals or as a group, tackles our culture's biggest ethical and social dilemmas, including hot topics such as street violence, abortion, autism, genocide, and stem cell research. www.joniandfriends.org/store/
- **FRIENDSHIP MINISTRIES** provide models for ministry to people with cognitive impairments. www.friendship.org

WOUNDED WARRIORS are another important group of people with visible and invisible disabilities. Tens of thousands of brave soldiers have returned from Iraq and Afghanistan bearing horrible wounds from their battle against terror. Marine captain Ryan Voltin, an attack-helicopter pilot, paid a dear price to serve our country when he suffered severe burns to his arms, head, and face. His left leg also had to be amputated. During his two years in the hospital, he underwent over 20 surgeries. He and his family endured challenges that would break most of us. But a turning point came when they attended a Wounded Warrior Getaway sponsored by Joni and Friends where they were able to open up and talk about their emotions for the first time with other military families. To learn more about how to support the **Wounded Warrior Project** visit www.woundedwarriorproject.org

"Join me in praying for our service men and women who are still fighting for freedom around the world," says Joni Eareckson Tada. "And for those disabled veterans who deserve our love and support."

What People with Disabilities Want You to Know

"**WHEN PEOPLE** look at me, they tend to think that I'm fragile or breakable because I have spina bifida. I may not be able to do certain things or participate in an activity, but I still want to be asked and included."

—**AMANDA**, *a college freshman*

"**SOME GUYS** make me feel like a loser because I don't drive and still live at home. My friend Adam lives with his parents too. But he understands and picks me up for church in his car."

—**JOSEPH**, *a baker's assistant with Asperger's and bipolar disorder*

"**SOMETIMES LIVING** with cerebral palsy is really difficult. I make it in the business world because I've learned how to trust God, and I've met so many people who have become great friends."

—**DARREN**, *a computer engineer*

"**I WISH OTHER KIDS** knew about the things I like, and all the things I can do. I would like to spend time with friends who like me for myself."

—**WILLIAM**, *a high school senior with intellectual and developmental disabilities*

"Don't just pretend to love others. Really love them. . . . Love each other with genuine affection, and take delight in honoring each other. . . . Be patient in trouble, and keep on praying. When God's people are in need, be ready to help them."

–ROMANS 12:9-13

TIPS FOR HELPING FRIENDS WITH DISABILITIES

- **LEARN** as much as you can about your friend's disability and look for creative ways to include him in your life and in the life of the community.
- **AVOID** making assumptions about the extent of your friend's limitations or abilities—when in doubt, ask!
- **MIND** your language! Remember that words are powerful and should be chosen carefully. The Life Span Institute at the University of Kansas created a set of guidelines for "people-first language" with input from over 100 disability organizations. For a copy visit www.lsi.ku.edu/~lsi/aboutus/guidelines.shtml.
- **OFFER** practical assistance, such as providing your friend with rides to and from the store, work, or medical appointments.
- **HELP** your friend navigate her way through the often confusing and sometimes overwhelming maze of government programs and services that may be available. See www.disability.gov for more information.
- **EDUCATE** yourself on difficult bioethical questions your friend might face, so that you can offer godly counsel when she needs it most.

The challenges and barriers many people with disabilities face can leave them isolated, alone and impoverished. Jesus understood this and purposefully modeled outreach to those with disabilities, those society considered outcasts. But he didn't stop there! In Luke 14:15–24, he tells a parable of a man who prepared a feast that was spurned by his invited guests. The man commanded his servant: "Go quickly into the streets and alleys of the town and invite the poor, the crippled, the blind, and the lame."

When we share our time, our energy, our resources, with those who have disabilities, we honor them and we honor our Savior (Matthew 25:40). We can bring tremendous help and hope through the simple act of friendship.

DEPENDING ON the severity of their impairment, people with disabilities (of any type) may differ in their experiences of and perspectives on their faith. Some may question God's sovereignty and need a supportive church to show them acceptance and love as they grow to trust God. Your friend's hope in the gospel may be restored as you faithfully walk alongside him or her.

- **KATHY** has multiple sclerosis and lives in a nursing home. She reached out to Joni and Friends in desperation: "All I want to do is just to have someone call me . . . someone to talk to." Kathy was connected with a volunteer. A friendship was forged through their phone conversations and now Kathy gets weekly visits from her friend to help her wash her hair.
- **JENNIFER** has cerebral palsy and was overcome with loneliness and discouragement. A caring friend took the time with Jennifer to search through Scriptures that showed God's love for her and then prayed with her, asking God to fill her void. Just a few weeks later, Jennifer had signed up to volunteer at a local center for kids with cerebral palsy. She loved her job of going from crib to crib, picking up the little ones in diapers and just loving on them. With the help of a friend, Jennifer found the answer to her prayer and her loneliness: loving others with cerebral palsy.

- **IF YOUR FRIEND** is dealing with a newly acquired disability, help him to find new ways of engaging in activities he's always enjoyed. For example, virtually every sport imaginable has been adapted to enable people with disabilities to participate. From basketball to mountain climbing, from football to golf—the possibilities are nearly endless!
- **ABOVE ALL,** extend grace to your friend with a disability. Remember that adjusting to newly acquired disabilities, or even new limitations associated with long-term disabilities, can take time. Be patient and reassure your friend that you will walk with her through the ups and downs of life with a disability . . . *no matter what.*

"Sometimes my co-workers don't invite me to go shopping or on picnics. They just assume that I can't cook, but I can. I also like playing cards with a large-print deck and being the score keeper."

—MARIA, A SINGLE MOTHER WITH VISUAL IMPAIRMENT

STEPS FOR PRAYING WITH FRIENDS WITH DISABILITIES

PEOPLE WITH DISABILITIES have the same spiritual needs as people without disabilities. They need to know the truths of the Bible and that they were uniquely created by God for a divine purpose. They can learn how to have a relationship with God through his Son, Jesus, as well as with a caring faith community. People with disabilities enjoy being invited to pray for others and to use their spiritual gifts in acts of service. Even those with limited intellectual abilities can understand the difference between right and wrong—and being truly loved or merely tolerated. While their bodies may be impaired, their souls are not.

Be a good listener. Listen to friends who share their concerns and fears. Listen to God as you ask him to show you how to pray for this person's specific needs, which may be as simple as a request for a peaceful night's sleep or for a pending diagnosis.

After you've listened, politely ask your friend if this is a good time to pray with her. Observe her body language as well as her words. Offer to come by at another time if you feel any hesitation on her part.

When friends struggle in their attempts to pray, assure them that a loving God understands their every thought, as well as their pain and suffering. God hears the faintest whisper.

"You know what I long for, Lord; you hear my every sigh." —PSALM 38:9

CHILDREN WITH SPECIAL NEEDS have their own unique challenges: stares in public, bullies at school, fear of doctors, and questions without answers. Yet many families do a wonderful job of helping children develop a strong sense of self-worth and a godly character. Thanks to the Internet, a number of websites offer interactive virtual communities and informative videos for children with disabilities. Kids' Corner is a go-to place on the web where there's always plenty of fun and interesting stuff to learn. It's an outstanding place to recommend to children's teachers and friends whose children have special needs. www.joniandfriends.org/kids-corner

"We can rejoice, too, when we run into problems and trials, for we know that they help us develop endurance. And endurance develops strength of character, and character strengthens our confident hope of salvation. And this hope will not lead to disappointment. For we know how dearly God loves us, because he has given us the Holy Spirit to fill our hearts with his love." —ROMANS 5:3–5

[3] See the Slaight Family's story at www.joniandfriends.org/television/tragedy-triumph/

FRIENDS CAN BE THE ARMS OF JESUS WHEN DISABILITY STRIKES

THE SLAIGHT FAMILY'S LIFE was forever changed when an oncoming car traveling at 90 miles per hour hit their van. One minute Jim and Janet were looking forward to summer vacation with their four children, and the next they were being whisked away in separate ambulances, leaving behind the lifeless body of their four-year-old. At the scene, Janet regained consciousness long enough to hear her oldest daughter crying and to see emergency responders kneeling near the wreckage, weeping. All she could do was call out to God.

God answered by sending their church family to assist them at every turn, especially since the parents' injuries required months of hospitalization. Friends stayed by the children's bedsides, shopped, cooked, and did laundry. Two of the children were paralyzed, never to walk again. But the Slaights' faith in God became the foundation on which they slowly rebuilt their lives.

Hannah, a teenager at the time, refused to let her paralysis keep her down. When it was time to get her driver's license, Hannah spent two hours in the hot sun lifting and pulling her body from her wheelchair to independently get in and out of the driver's seat. Her younger brother Joe, who is also a paraplegic, says that he and Hannah share a deeper connection than most siblings because they understand one another on good days—and bad.

Hannah is grateful that God has put amazing people in her life that she may never have met without the accident—people who've helped to make her the person she is today.[3]

Pray specifically and with assurance that God hears and answers prayer. Whether we feel weak or strong in our prayers, our hope is built on the promises of God.

"LORD, you know the hopes of the helpless. Surely you will hear their cries and comfort them."

—PSALM 10:17

Give thanks for a life worth living. Joni Eareckson Tada has said, "Life worth living is not found in a set of circumstances—whether pleasant or painful. Life worth living is found in a Person, the Prince of Life. The Resurrection and the Life. Jesus is the Way, the Truth and the Life. He has words of life. And the moments we invest in praying for his will to be done in lives, communities, and even nations will extend beyond this life—and beyond time itself."

DISABILITIES CAN BUILD CHARACTER

LIKE A LOT of children and adults with attention deficit disorder and dyslexia, Shaw Bates struggled to succeed in school, to make friends, and generally to feel good about himself. Thanks to the support of his family and his love for God, Shaw was able to graduate from Biola University with a B.A. in Psychology and go on to become a Community Support Specialist at Goodwill Industries of Hawaii.

In a 2014 Joni and Friends radio interview, Shaw shared how he felt growing up in order to encourage young people to never give up: "When I was young, I wish someone would have said to me, 'Hey, I know you're different, but I'll be your friend.' Learning for me was like climbing a ladder, while people without disabilities took the escalator. Math was like a foreign language, but I had good teachers who really cared about me. When I was seventeen, I didn't know what God wanted me to do with my life. In prayer I felt the Lord saying he wanted me to make a difference in other people's lives and to serve him in full-time Christian ministry. I figured that if God would powerfully use Moses, he could use me too."

BEATITUDES FOR FRIENDS OF PEOPLE WITH DISABILITIES[2]

Blessed are you who take the time to listen to difficult speech, for you help me to know that if I persevere I can be understood.

Blessed are you who never bid me to "hurry up," for I often need time rather than help.

Blessed are you who stand beside me as I enter new and untried ventures, for my failures will be outweighed by the times I surprise myself and you.

Blessed are you who ask for my help, for my greatest need is to be needed.

Blessed are you who understand that it is difficult for me to put my thoughts into words.

Blessed are you who, with a smile, encourage me to try once more.

Blessed are you who never remind me that I sometimes ask the same question several times.

Blessed are you who respect me and love me as I am, not as you wish I were.

---

[2] http://www.joniandfriends.org/media/uploads/downloads/Beatitudes.pdf

Aspire Press, an imprint of Rose Publishing, LLC
www.hendricksonrose.com

 020718SCG

AspirePress

Product code: 4164X

RELIGION/Christian Life/Personal Growth

ISBN 978-1-62862-475-5

9 781628 624755

Joni and Friends
INTERNATIONAL DISABILITY CENTER

Photos on pages 2, 3, 10, 13 used with permission of Joni and Friends.

Retailers 5-pack 4168X ISBN: 9781628624816